THERE'S NO SUCH THING AS CLOSING THE DEAL.

A BRIEF(CASE)
GUIDE TO
SUCCESSFUL
SALES

Jane Murphy

ISBN: 0615591124
ISBN-13: 978-0-615-59112-4

CONTENTS

HELP! I'M DROWNING IN SALES TRAINING!

INTRODUCTION

As you pick up this book, I imagine there are dozens of others doing the same. Some will put it back on the shelf, but a few of you will head to the checkout. That's good, because you're the ones I'm speaking to. If you have a few minutes to invest in your sales career, I've got a book of bullets that gets to the point quickly and allows for easy execution. (Did I really put 'bullets' and 'execution' in the same sentence? Sorry.)

How many books on sales technique did you pick up before this one? I've spent nearly 30 years managing, training and selling. In that time, I've attempted to read at least that many sales training books. I've never found one that was simple, direct and so useful I wanted to keep it in my back pocket or briefcase for easy reference. One that I could pull out when I was sitting on the phone, waiting and nervous, to help me focus on the basics of selling.

Over the years, I've watched hundreds of salespeople suc- ceed or fail. What would have increased their odds of success? What do *you* need to do to succeed in sales? This book takes all my observations and packages them in an easy-to-use, friendly format. I won't make you read about cheese or six of something or spend 300 pages finding out how to close a deal in five minutes. Because I want you to be selling, not reading.

If you take a few points from every section, I guarantee you'll be a better salesperson than you are today, whether you're new to the field or someone like me, who has had a successful career but can appreciate a quick review on the fundamentals.

Are you with me? Good. Move on and have fun.

PART 1

WHAT DO YOU MEAN – THERE'S NO SUCH THING AS CLOSING THE DEAL?

TO EXPLAIN, TRY YOUR HAND AT THIS TRUE AND FALSE QUIZ:

1. **Success in sales is a numbers game.**

    FALSE. It's a conversation game.

2. **Sales is about lunches with prospects.**

    FALSE. Unless they'll be giving you a big sale that day, you've wasted hours.

3. **Sales is about adapting to your prospect.**

    FALSE. Sales is about building trust by bringing your unique self to the conversation, not the person you think they want.

4. **I can take rejection.**

    FALSE. Most people can't, including good salespeople. But they can shake it off, laugh about it or believe it's not about them.

5. **Sales is about using a few simple rules.**

    TRUE. These rules help all of us hopelessly undisciplined human beings perform like focused athletes.

1

6. Sales is like factory work.

> TRUE. Those who understand this point execute the process with repetitive tasks and behavior.

7. A sale is successful because of the product.

> FALSE. As you know, a lot of bad products are sold every day. A sale is about having someone trust you enough to partner with you.

8. Salespeople are successful because they have great personalities.

> FALSE. Frankly, I've met some successful salespeople who are downright nutty, but they are good at the points above.

DO YOU SEE ANYTHING THERE ABOUT CLOSING THE DEAL?

No. That's because you'll never get to a deal if you haven't focused on the elements highlighted in the quiz—conversation, trust, repeated behavior, simple rules, and good humor. If you lose a sale, don't blame it on the closing. Blame it on a failure to execute on these points from the very opening of your relationship with the prospect.

PART 2

DON'T MAKE ME PICK UP THE PHONE!

COLD CALLING THAT ACTUALLY WORKS.

Cold calling is successful because you strategized before you picked up the phone. You're going to get a few good opportunities. Do everything you can to maximize those opportunities.

- Know when you're at your best during the day. Are you a morning person? Better in the afternoon? Use that time to do your focused cold calls. If you're not on your game, you'll miss opportunities. Play to your strengths by calling when you're at your sharpest.

- A sale is about conversations. Set a goal everyday for conversations—at least six. (That's not six dials. The only purpose for dials is conversations.) Once you hit the goal, STOP. It's important to stay fresh so you don't miss opportunities while on a call. Sales momentum grows to a point and then drops off dramatically. If you keep going once you've hit your stretch goal for the day, the next few conversations won't have the same strength and you may squander opportunities.

- As you proceed toward your goal for the day, you get better with each call. The minute you break your momentum you are back to square one. Block short time periods, maybe two to three hours, and don't stop between calls. If you have a good rhythm from consistent calling in a tight period of time, you will spot the opportunities and hit the winner.

KNOW WHO'S WHO.

- Focus a lot of time choosing and fine tuning your prospect list. Like factory work, sales start with raw material. The better that material, the more successful the product will be. Look for a list that no one else is using. If you're not following the pack, you might find opportunities with less competition.

- Concentrate on two criteria: Where do I have the best shot? Where can I make the most money?

- Call the most senior person you should be contacting. If you're afraid to talk to him or her, you're in the wrong field. Even if you have to work your way down, it's good to reference the most senior person as the reason for your call when you talk to the next person in the chain.

- Selling is not about making one phone call and moving on. If you don't have a good contact, or they're not available and you're speaking to someone else—anyone else—use it. It's an opportunity to improve your list by checking facts or asking questions. Once you do speak to your contact, you'll be that much more prepared for success.

REJECTION. IT'S GOING TO HAPPEN A LOT.

Make it funny. Seriously. Here are some tricks:

- Play a game with a friend who's also in sales. Most rejections buys dinner or drinks.

- Play the odds. It's a math problem. You have to have so many rejections in order to get a winner. Keep count of your rejections and you'll know when you're close to success.

- If the prospect hangs up on you, call back and apologize for getting disconnected. When one call turns around like that in a day, you'll feel triumphant.

Remember, if you don't get some rejections, you can't get any wins. Don't let rejections be your excuse to throw in the towel. Somebody made a lot of money by saying 'no pain, no gain.' So celebrate your incremental victories: You played the odds today and you're one day closer to a win.

A WORD ABOUT GATEKEEPERS.

You know, it's that person who's supposed to keep you away from the person you want to talk to. (For this discussion, let's say it's a 'she.')

- DO NOT BE AFRAID. Remember, she has a job to do, just like you. Appreciate what she does but do not show fear. The confidence in your voice and your conviction about why you need to get through will win out most of the time.

- Ask for your contact by first name. If you convey a sense of familiarity, the gatekeeper will think there is already a connection.

- When she asks who is calling, answer simply with your name and firm. Keep that confidence in your voice.

- If you start to lose the battle—maybe hearing the death question, 'Will they know what this is about?'—do this: deflect the question, compose yourself, then answer honestly. Why? Deflecting the question—with a question back, humor or a reference to an unrelated subject, maybe about the city, something in the news, or even a funny story of about you—takes the air out of her question. You get a chance to gain control of the conversation. If that fails, simply ask to be put through to voicemail and call again another time.

- When you call back and get the gatekeeper again, reference your previous call, honestly and with some humor. She is human and—over time—confidence, politeness and humor will win her over.

- Don't run for the hills when you encounter tough gatekeepers. Set a goal: Today I will win over one of them. Remember, everyone who calls is having the same problem. Those who are politely persistent and patient could win big, because if you get past a good gatekeeper, you know there are very few of your competitors talking with those decision-makers.

A MESSAGE ABOUT MESSAGES.

- It's the great debate: Should you leave a message or not? Sure, but not more than once every two weeks. More than that could be considered stalking.

- Option 1: Casual. Use the prospect's first name and simply state your name, company and cell number.

- Option 2: Casual Plus. To the above information, add a quick sentence on why you're calling.

- Don't tell your company's life story, or your own, for that matter. People start to lose interest if the message goes on too long. And besides—if you've given them all the information on voice mail, they have no reason to call you back.

PART 3

> ## HOLY ?@#!
> ## I HAVE THE
> ## PROSPECT ON
> ## THE PHONE!

After much cold calling, you're getting ready to leave yet another message and—WHAM!—a live voice is on the other end and it's exactly the person you want. These opportunities are few, so you must be ready. How do you maximize—or otherwise stated, not !@#?-up—this moment?

EASY DOES IT.

- Don't rush into the call. Remember, the prospect wasn't expecting to talk with you, so take a moment to ease both of you into the dialog. The last thing you want is a prospect fleeing from the crazy person (you) who has launched into a bizarre sales pitch or (even worse) asked how his day is and all he's thinking is, *It was fine until I picked up this call.*

- If you start politely and slowly, the prospect won't feel threatened and you'll have time to collect your thoughts after hours of leaving messages.

9

- Here's an example of pacing a call. "Hi, this is YOUR NAME from YOUR COMPANY. I'm sorry, I was expecting to get your voicemail. Do you have time now?"

- Most will give you a few minutes and now it's make it or break it. This is what you need to prepare for, because if you succeed past this step, you have a legitimate sales process in place.

- It's easy to choke. The best way to avoid it is to practice. Write out your lead-in—hopefully just one short line—and a few key questions to get the conversation going. Use it every time and it will flow naturally.

- The lead-in should be a few words that frame the call, so the prospect doesn't think she is now trapped for life. Make it broad enough that she doesn't have the opportunity to shut you down over the details. For example: "I represent YOUR SERVICE OR YOUR PRODUCT, and just wanted to connect with you quickly to see about starting a conversation over the next few months about your needs and our services."

PROSPECTS, ON AVERAGE, WILL BE HOSTILE.

- Accept this now and move on. You might be hostile too if a stranger called to talk about something you hadn't planned on discussing today.

- If this frustrates or scares you, get out of the business now. As a sales person, your job is to overcome this hostility and turn the call around. This is the first step on every call you'll make.

- It's not hard if you treat it as a planned process. You know it's coming so prepare your responses to typical hostile walls, wait for them to happen and execute.

- Here are examples of hostile walls: 1) I don't talk to strangers. 2) I'm too busy right now. 3) I already have YOUR PRODUCT.

- Take these and other examples and write out your responses. Don't think them through, but just write out what comes immediately into your mind, no matter how odd, funny or rude. This is your personality coming through. Authentic, unique responses will throw the prospect off guard because he is expecting a bland business reply. Instead, you have countered with something different. Great. You now have a small window to engage. Jump through it with a non-traditional question to elicit conversation.

QUESTIONS: MAKE THEM INTERESTING.

- No one will stay on the phone with a sales person who drills them up front with silly or detailed questions.

- Think about when you meet someone new in your personal life. Say you're standing next to a stranger at a party and you decide to strike up a conversation. If you ask questions that are too pointed, talk about yourself or babble without taking a breath, the stranger will flee. So will your prospect.

- Instead, think of simple, interesting, non-threatening questions that offer an opportunity for the person to respond back with more than four words. Ask yourself these questions before you ever get on the phone. If you can answer them in less than four words, your prospects will shoot for two and you won't engage them.

- A good question has an answer that you're interested in. This will lead to conversation.

- Try this trick: If you want to find how the prospect is using the product you are selling, first think about how everyone else asks that question. Then change it. Don't be typical.

- Here are typical business-speak questions that everybody uses and you should avoid at all cost:
  - Can I update you about *PRODUCT*?
  - Are you the decision-maker?
  - Do you have *PRODUCT*?
  - When was the last time you changed vendors?
  - Are you familiar with our services or product?

- Now, here are some un-typical and more interesting questions that will create conversation:
  - How many sales calls have you already taken today?
  - I would like to talk to you about *PRODUCT*. What would be the best way to approach this dialog?

You'll find a list of these and other questions at the end of this book for easy reference.

BODY LANGUAGE.

Believe it or not, you can hear it through the phone. Listen to your prospect's body language and map out your response.

- A pause. This could be good or bad. Proceed quickly to a question that produces conversation or an answer longer than four words.

- A sigh. Check in. You are losing him. Politely ask to keep going and then proceed to an interesting question.

- A deep breath. Be aggressive. Call it out: "I can tell I haven't started out well. How can I start this again?"

- A laugh. You've got her. Move forward.

PART 4

OMG! I'M IN CONVERSATION. NOW WHAT DO I DO?

Congratulations! You survived the first two minutes of a near-death experience with the prospect. You've framed the call, been given permission to move forward, and asked a few interesting questions to start the process.

BE GOAL-ORIENTED.

- There are two simple goals for this first call. Once you achieve them hang up, or you could end up blowing it by over-dialoguing. Too many words are usually a bigger spoiler than too few.

- GOAL 1: Make sure you're talking with the right decision-maker and don't be afraid to push this point. Time is your investment and spending time with the wrong person earns you nothing. If you're talking with the wrong person, at least get information before you let him go.

- GOAL 2: If you have the right person, progress the call until you get a commitment for a next meeting.

- Maximize the opportunity, even if you're tired, sick, or want to go home. Push yourself. Measure your push by not hanging up until you get three 'no's' from the prospect. If you do that—regardless of the outcome—you know you maximized the opportunity.

TALK YOUR WAY TO THE FINISH.

- Avoid sales speak. Focus on conversation, not on framing the question right or making sure you ask open-ended questions. We don't think or act like this in an interpersonal environment. If you spoke like that, you would be considered odd.

- Talk to your prospect the way you would talk to anyone you just met. He will continue the conversation if he likes you and senses he can trust you. So don't leave out a key ingredient: YOUR PERSONALITY.

- Finish with two strong questions that are interesting and actually provoke thought from the prospect. This is a time to share some information between you. Select something from the list of questions at the end of this book.

MAKE A DATE.

- The clock is ticking. This first call was unplanned for the prospect. Don't overstay your welcome. Finish with a request for more conversation. Here are some examples:

- I know you're busy. Could we continue this conversation further?

- I've enjoyed discussing where your needs are now. Could we keep this dialog going?

- Pick a time and ask for a meeting. Politely ask again. If you're still not getting what you want, ask again. If all else fails, go for the final ask—"Can I keep in touch?"—and pick a time you'll call next. Never let the prospect determine your next call or move. Drive her to the time that you set up.

- Always end by thanking her for her time.

PART 5

OK, THE CALL WAS EASY. BUT NOW I'VE GOT TO MEET WITH HIM!

THE FIRST CALL GETS YOU IN THE DOOR. THE SECOND GETS YOU AN INVITATION TO STAY FOR DINNER.

- The second call has two goals: First, create an atmosphere where the prospect wants to hear more. Second, orchestrate the next contact.

- Do your homework. Look for people you know who might have a connection with the Board of Directors, the CFO or the owner of the company. Ask them for information or to put in a good word about you.

DISTINGUISH YOURSELF.

- Presentations don't create connections. Personality does. Be yourself, not simply a presenter.

- Plan on being different than the pack. Take risks, so you are not like everyone else.

- People buy good products, but they also buy bad products.

The reason? They connected with the seller.

- You ingrain yourself because the prospect thinks you're interesting or smart or funny or full of helpful knowledge. It's how you build relationships, whether they're personal or professional. If you keep that foremost in your mind, your prospects will trust you because they know you're sincere. They are meeting you, not your product.

- Keep the participants off guard by holding a meeting that is not the 'same old, same old.' Make it feel like a meeting you want to go to. Interesting. Fun.

- When you leave, you want the participants to be talking not about the positives of your product, but about you. If they like you, you'll be invited back.

DON'T JUST SLIDE THROUGH.

- A sale is a slow, well-planned process. You take baby steps to move the sale forward. If you tell your whole story and demand their interest, they have no reason to dance with you again.

- Many salespeople run through a presentation like a weird video game. The presentation should be a grounding to keep the conversation moving in an organized fashion. They should be listening to you, not flipping through to see what's next.

- Memorize each slide so you can maintain eye contact with the people in the room. You are an actor. Learn your lines so you can engage the audience.
- If you read your notes or recite a speech, like in 9th grade his-

tory class, you will not draw the audience in. They should be a part of this experience, not watching it unfold.

TURN A PRESENTATION TO A GROUP INTO A CONVERSATION.

- Prepare two questions for each slide. Use at least one or both if you sense interest on that page.

- Examples of questions during a presentation that are not interesting:
    - Any questions so far?
    - Does that make sense?
    - Is this what you're looking for?

- Interesting questions make people think; not just nod their heads, but actually talk. Try the questions on yourself. Write the answer on paper. You'll know they're boring if you're bored trying to answer them. Examples of interesting questions to ask during a presentation:
    - I ran through this slide quickly. Let's take a moment to get a sense of what was compelling from this information that I can highlight further.
    - Where do you feel you want to go next, now that we've covered this information?
    - This product continues to evolve. Where do you see improvements compared to what you are presently using?

- Most salespeople treat a presentation as, 'Me first, then you.' But that's not how an interesting conversation goes. It's a give and take. You tell a little, then you ask about them and they tell you a little. Nothing personal, but if it's all about you, it's boring.

- Selling is improvisation; you follow the lead of what was said before. A class at your local improvisational theater may be the best training for presentations.

DON'T LET PRESENTATIONS TO INDIVIDUALS OR GROUPS STALL.

- What if you ask questions and they don't answer? Stop and tell them your goal is to really understand them. Let them know you're not letting them off the hook, so they only get to listen. This is worth the risk because if you don't have their interest at that point, you've lost anyway. You have to get back on track. They need to be involved in the conversation, not observers of it. Don't be the sales person who ends up carrying both sides of the conversation. People who talk to themselves do not inspire confidence.

- If you get to your third slide and your audience is still just sitting there, nodding and listening, STOP. You're losing ground and going forward will gain you nothing. You've got to get the party started. DO SOMETHING UNEXPECTED. You have nothing to lose. For example:
   - Ask them to flip to the last page and then go backwards.
   - Tell them to give back the handout of the presentation. Pose one question and ask them write out an answer. Then use their answers for discussion. BE DIFFERENT. People remember different.

- Remind yourself that you're in charge of this group. Think of it as a training session, not a sales pitch.

- Once you feel that you have them engaged again, finish the presentation. Use one question per slide to keep conversation flowing.

- When the last slide is done, ask two final questions: What did I miss? What are you worried about? Don't ask any more questions.

WIND DOWN TO A PERFECT ENDING.

- At this point you need to strengthen your relationship with the prospect. Lighten the conversation. Shift the mood with unrelated questions to the audience, such as:
  - How long have each of you served on the board?
  - I meant to ask you: As I came in, I noticed the interesting architecture. Any history there?

- OR, if you're presenting to only one person and it's a manufacturer or other interesting environment, ask for a quick tour.

- OR, use humor to change the direction of the meeting. For example: "That is the conclusion of the presentation. We as a company also support the green movement. Would you please take a moment to eat the handouts?" You will get a stare, then a laugh. The point is, it's a shift. Something different.

- Finally, ask and really understand the next steps of their buying process. Don't leave until it makes sense, so that you don't end up running blind through the rest of the sales process.

PART 6

THE MEETING WENT WELL. WHY HAVEN'T THEY CALLED?

PROSPECTS DON'T CALL YOU. YOU ARE PAID TO CALL THEM.

- You are not the only thing on their minds. Reach out to keep you in their thoughts.

- Selling is a process. You should lay out a standard game plan for how you handle a prospect at every stage and execute it consistently. Success on this part of the sales cycle is all about process.

- After a meeting, send thank you notes to the participants. Make them handwritten. Because it's an art that has died, it will be more appreciated and stand out. It's polite to thank them for their time and this marketing touch will show them you care.

- The goal for this point in the process is to continue to deepen the relationship with key decision-makers.

- Build a roadmap of your strategy for the next six months. It should be a mix of touches: phone calls, face-to-face meetings, or maybe interesting articles. Execute your plan systematically and completely for best results. Don't cave in to feelings of loss, lack of confidence or indifference.

- In each interaction with the prospect, ask, "Why no?" or "Why not now?" Explain your willingness to wait, but emphasize your belief that this is his best option.

- Build a sense of familiarity with your prospect by referencing past conversations, discussing other interesting topics, like something relevant in the news, and generally showing interest in her as an individual, such as asking about a shared hobby. Everyone talks about weather and sports. Go for something different.

PERSISTENCE AND PATIENCE PAY OFF.

- Many salespeople back off at this point. Don't. This is where you show prospects you can really make a difference to them.

- Call every few months and leave voice mail messages. Remind them of who you are, that you're keeping in touch and you hope all is well.

- Try to get meetings at least once every four months.

- Repeat the process for all prospects with whom you had meetings. Repetition and consistent execution will get some of these prospects to convert.

- Sales success is about being with the prospect at the right time. Prospects buy when they are ready. If you've built a connection, you'll get their business.

- Failure is disorganization at this point. It's that simple.

REMIND ME AGAIN: WHAT DID YOU SAY?

THERE'S NO SUCH THING AS CLOSING THE DEAL.

Success in sales is about making a connection through constant contact. Telling your story as only you can tell it. Pushing for a relationship, not a sale. Playing the odds and making sure you're in the right place at the right time. It's simply about careful, repeated execution.

Think of the sales process as following a map. Like using the navigator on your phone, you set your start and finish points and then follow the route. If your prospect takes you off that route, your job is to get yourself back on the main road. If you visit a site off the route with a specific prospect, get right back on. Running a map allows you to control the process and avoid your prospect taking you down a rabbit hole you can't climb out of.

Actually create that map for yourself. Identify the stages and stops along the route (your sales process) and write out the purpose and the amount of time you want to spend at each stop.

Success in sales is based on how you begin and execute, not how you close. Now get started and good luck!

ABOUT THE AUTHOR

Jane Murphy held a number of senior sales and management positions during a 20-year career with Fidelity Investments, as well as being one of the senior managers who was asked to conduct sales training for the client services teams. Her last role was as senior vice president overseeing a large national division that sold 401K services to small and medium-sized companies. She established the division in 1995 with one salesperson and annual sales of less than $100,000 and grew it to a large organization with more than 80 people and sales of more than $2 billion in new assets every year.

Using the experience of 30 years in the corporate world, Murphy started her own boutique firm, Acceleration Retirement, which specializes in sales, marketing consulting, training, and execution of growth strategies for select clients. The company, with more than 20 associates, has seen exponential revenue growth over the last two years and is considered a one of the top tier firms for quality execution.

Over the years, Murphy has hired and trained hundreds of salespeople. She began to formulate and use the methods in this book in her days as a young sales manager and continued to develop and fine tune these ideas as her career progressed. The methods are based on observing successful and struggling salespeople and the fundamental tools she used over the years to develop herself, her organization and her successful sales staff.

A QUICK GUIDE TO QUESTIONS

☐ How many sales calls have you already taken today?

☐ I would like to talk to you about [PRODUCT/SERVICE]. What would be the best way to approach this dialog?

☐ Can you give me a quick update on the status of [PRODUCT/SERVICE] in your business?

☐ I know we only have a few minutes. How can I best update you on our services? Or changes in the market?

☐ How has your company's life cycle changed since you adopted this [PRODUCT/SERVICE]?

☐ Internally, have you discussed the next generation of this [PRODUCT/SERVICE]?

☐ What changes are you focused on now to reach your goals for this year and next?

☐ How have you traditionally connected with your vendors?

☐ What do you see as future trends in your industry?

☐ Have you had time to look at future trends for this [PRODUCT/SERVICE]?

- [ ] Where are you in the life cycle of your business?

- [ ] What precipitates you analyzing your [PRODUCT/SERVICE] platform?

- [ ] When you set up this program, what was the original goal?

- [ ] Is the structure still meeting that goal?

- [ ] What is your process for reviewing your [PRODUCT/SERVICE] platforms?

- [ ] Have you been able to document and review the lift you've seen from implantation of this [PRODUCT/SERVICE]?

- [ ] What is your goal for attracting and retaining employees?

- [ ] What were some of the items you focused on the last time you changed this [PRODUCT/SERVICE]?

- [ ] As you can see, the service model continues to evolve. Where do you see improvements, compared to how you are structured now?

- [ ] How can I best add value in the limited time we have?

NOTES

NOTES

www.ingramcontent.com/pod-product-compliance
Lightning Source LLC
Chambersburg PA
CBHW070921210326
41521CB00010B/2276